AWESOME
Bible Verses
Every Kid
Should Know

Rebecca Lutzer

HARVEST HOUSE PUBLISHERS
EUGENE, OREGON

Cover by Left Coast Design, Portland, Oregon
Illustrations © Krieg Barrie

AWESOME BIBLE VERSES EVERY KID SHOULD KNOW

Copyright © 2013 by Rebecca Lutzer
Published by Harvest House Publishers
Eugene, Oregon 97402
www.harvesthousepublishers.com

Library of Congress Cataloging-in-Publication Data
Lutzer, Rebecca.
Awesome Bible verses every kid should know / Rebecca Lutzer.
    p. cm.
ISBN 978-0-7369-3938-6 (pbk.)
ISBN 978-0-7369-4128-0 (eBook)
1. Bible—Study and teaching (Elementary) 2. Bible—Children's use. 3. Bible—Memorizing. I. Title.
BS618.L88 2013
220—dc23
                                                                2012035428

Printed in the United States of America
                18 19 20 21 / BP-JH / 10 9

This book is lovingly dedicated
to my delightful grandchildren, whom I love dearly

Jack ~ Samuel ~ Emma ~ Anna ~ Abigail ~ Owen ~ Evelyn ~ Isaac

with my earnest prayer that you will
delight in the law of the Lord and think about it often
(Psalm 1:2)

Contents

Introduction

Hi, kids!

The Bible is like a huge treasure chest, full of wonderful truths that help us in many ways. The Bible tells us about God, how we began, the world, how we should behave, and how we can please God. It teaches us what is wrong and what is right, corrects us when we are wrong, encourages us to do the right thing, comforts us when we're sad, and tells us about Jesus and how much He loves us.

God gave us the Bible because He loves us and wants us to know Him.

I'm so excited to share some of my favorite Bible verses with you! I hope you will memorize them and learn what they mean. This is one of the most important things you can ever do.

Hiding God's Word in our hearts gives us the strength to say no when we are tempted to disobey His rules. It helps us to be kind and to love and forgive others. When you memorize God's Word, you can think about it whenever you want to. It's like a good friend who is always with you. A righteous person delights in the law of the Lord and meditates on it day and night (Psalm 1:2).

Hebrews 4:12 tells us what the Bible is like:

- It is alive and active, filled with power and life.

- It is sharper than a double-edged sword, reaching down into our soul and spirit.

- It judges the thoughts and attitudes of our hearts, helping us to believe and do the right things.

As you read this book, you will find that each chapter teaches you something important about God, yourself, and others. As you memorize the selected verses, you will also learn what they are teaching. This is called theology. It is important that you not only know the verses but also know what they mean. This knowledge will always be with you to help you understand God, yourself, and how to get along with others. It will help you make good decisions throughout your life.

Are you ready to begin? Memorizing is hard work, so I'm praying that you will stick to it and keep trying until you have memorized every verse in this book. Then your heart and mind will be filled with powerful words that will help you every day. I'm praying that you will grow to love God and His Word with all your heart!

You are a special kid who can sing, "Jesus loves me, this I know, for the Bible tells me so." And I love you too!

Rebecca Lutzer

AWESOME
Bible Verses
Every Kid
Should Know

God

Psalm 77:13
Your ways, God, are holy. What god is as great as our God?

Psalm 90:2
Before the mountains were born or you brought forth the whole world, from everlasting to everlasting you are God.

Isaiah 40:25,28
"To whom will you compare me? Or who is my equal?" says the Holy One...Do you not know? Have you not heard? The LORD is the everlasting God, the Creator of the ends of the earth. He will not grow tired or weary, and his understanding no one can fathom.

John 1:18
No one has ever seen God, but the one and only Son, who is himself God and is in closest relationship with the Father, has made him known.

God is the supreme being in the universe. He has always existed. No one created Him. He knows everything, He can be everywhere, and He is stronger than anyone or anything in the world. He is the highest in rank and authority. He is holy and perfect, and He cannot do anything wrong.

What I Think

- Since I can't see God, how do I know He is real?
- Where does He live?
- Why do some people believe God isn't real?

What God Wants Me to Know

1. There is only one God, but He has three persons: God the Father, God the Son (Jesus), and God the Holy Spirit. Each person of God has different roles, but He is all the same God. God is the *Trinity*, which means He is three in one.

2. God created everything. "In the beginning, God created the heavens and the earth" (Genesis 1:1).

3. No one can see God because He is a spirit. And besides, He is holy and very different from the people He created.

4. God loves us and wants us to know Him.

5. We don't know exactly where God lives, but the Bible says He dwells beyond the heavens (1 Kings 8:27). He can be in the bottom of the deepest ocean and out by the farthest star at the same time. He can be everywhere at once!

Look at It This Way...

To understand a little more how God is three persons in one being, think about an egg. It is only one egg, but it has three parts—the shell, the white, and the yolk. An egg is not an egg without all three parts. Each part needs the other to form the egg. In the same way, there is only one God, but He has three persons—the Father, the Son, and the Spirit. Each person needs the other to form the Trinity.

Prayer

Dear God,

Even though I don't understand everything about You, please help me to honor, respect, worship, love, and obey You. I want to learn as much as I can about You from the Bible because You are awesome! Amen.

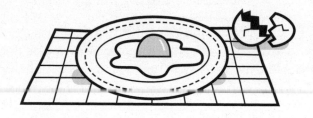

Creation

Genesis 1:1,27,31

In the beginning God created the heavens and the earth...God created mankind in his own image, in the image of God he created them; male and female he created them...God saw all that he had made, and it was very good.

Nehemiah 9:6

You alone are the LORD. You made the heavens, even the highest heavens, and all their starry host, the earth and all that is on it, the seas and all that is in them. You give life to everything, and the multitudes of heaven worship you.

John 1:3

Through him all things were made; without him nothing was made that has been made.

A long time ago, nothing existed. Nothing, that is, except God. There were no stars, no planets, and no other living things. Everything was dark and empty. Then God spoke and created everything. He told the planets, the sun, the moon, the stars, and everything on them to come into being. He made it all out of nothing! Then He made the first man and woman. Only God could do such a miracle. He tells us how He did it in the first book of the Bible—Genesis, which means "beginning."

What I Think

- If God hadn't made people, He would have had the whole universe to Himself.

- I'm glad God made people so we could know Him.

- God must be bigger than the universe.

What God Wants Me to Know

1. God's words have so much power that when He spoke, the whole universe was created—sun, moon, stars, oceans, trees and plants, birds, and everything that lives in the water or on the land.

2. Then God made a beautiful garden called Eden. Next He created the first man, whose name was Adam, and the first woman, whose name was Eve. God put them in the garden to take care of it. Everything God created was perfect.

3. The wonderful things God made remind us of how great He is (Psalm 8:1; 19:1; Romans 1:20).

4. Some people don't believe God created the world and everything in it. For example, some people believe that living things just happened all on their own and that these living things eventually turned into people. This theory is called *evolution*. Of course, no one can prove it.

Look at It This Way...

A Christian man was talking with someone who didn't believe that God exists (an atheist). The atheist believed that the universe was not created by God, but that it just happened to come together all by itself.

The Christian asked, "Do you think your wristwatch could have made itself without somebody putting it together? Could the different parts have just appeared and organized themselves on their own to work perfectly?"

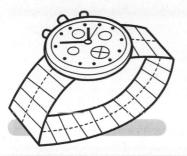

The atheist was silent for a moment but then admitted that a wristwatch needed a designer—a person who was smart enough to make the different pieces and put them together.

Believing that little bits of metal formed a wristwatch on their own is even harder than believing that our complicated universe just appeared and came together all by itself. The Bible tells us that God is the Creator of everything. We can always believe that what God tells us about Himself is true.

Prayer

Dear God,

Thank You for making such a wonderful world. I don't understand exactly how You did it, but I believe Your words, and I know I can always trust You. Amen.

Jesus

Matthew 1:21-23

"She will give birth to a son, and you are to give him the name Jesus, because he will save his people from their sins." All this took place to fulfill what the Lord had said through the prophet: "The virgin will conceive and give birth to a son, and they will call him Immanuel" (which means "God with us").

John 1:1-3

In the beginning was the Word, and the Word was with God, and the Word was God. He was with God in the beginning. Through him all things were made; without him nothing was made that has been made.

Acts 4:10,12

It is by the name of Jesus Christ of Nazareth, whom you crucified but whom God raised from the dead, that this man stands before you healed... Salvation is found in no one else, for there is no other name under heaven given to mankind by which we must be saved.

Jesus is God. Jesus is also called the Son of God. He is the second person of the Godhead. Jesus left His home in heaven and was born into the human race so He could be both God and man. Then He was willing to die on the cross for us so that our sins could be forgiven. That is why He is called the Savior. Jesus loves us and wants to be our friend.

What I Think

- I love Jesus, and I wish I could see Him.

- Sometimes I feel sad that Jesus had to die on the cross.

- Where is Jesus now?

- Can I live with Jesus when I die?

What God Wants Me to Know

1. In the beginning, before anything else existed, Jesus was with God, and He was God.

2. Jesus is the Creator. He made everything.

3. Jesus has many names, such as Son of God, Savior, Lord, Christ, the Word, Messiah, Wonderful Counselor, Mighty God, and Prince of Peace.

4. Jesus is also called the God-man. When He was born as a baby in Bethlehem, He was still God, but He was also a human. He wanted to be part of the human race so He could die on the cross for our sins. Then He rose from the dead—that's called the resurrection—and went back to live in heaven.

5. Jesus is perfect. He never sinned or did anything wrong.

Look at It This Way...

A famous student of the Bible was asked what the most important message of the Bible was. This was his answer: "Jesus loves me, this I know, for the Bible tells me so." Here are more words to this wonderful song.

Jesus loves me, this I know,
for the Bible tells me so.
Little ones to Him belong;
they are weak, but He is strong.

Jesus loves me when I'm good,
when I do the things I should.
Jesus loves me when I'm bad,
though it makes Him very sad.

Jesus loves me, He who died,
heaven's gates to open wide;
He will wash away my sin,
let His little child come in.

Yes, Jesus loves me, yes, Jesus loves me,
Yes, Jesus loves me, the Bible tells me so.

Prayer

Dear Jesus,

Thank You for loving me so much and dying on the cross to forgive my sins. I love You, and I want to obey You all the time. Please watch over me every day and keep me safe. Amen.

The Holy Spirit

John 14:25-26

All this I have spoken while still with you. But the Advocate, the Holy Spirit, whom the Father will send in my name, will teach you all things and will remind you of everything I have said to you.

Romans 8:26-27

The Spirit helps us in our weakness. We do not know what we ought to pray for, but the Spirit himself intercedes for us through wordless groans. And he who searches our hearts knows the mind of the Spirit, because the Spirit intercedes for God's people in accordance with the will of God.

Galatians 5:22-23

The fruit of the Spirit is love, joy, peace, forbearance, kindness, goodness, faithfulness, gentleness and self-control.

God exists as three persons in one being, the Trinity—Father, Son, and Holy Spirit. That means the Holy Spirit is God. The Spirit gave Jesus the power to offer Himself on the cross, and the Spirit raised Him from the dead. Even though the Spirit is invisible, He has knowledge, feelings, and great power. The Holy Spirit is important to us and assures us that we belong to God. He enables us to be kind and helpful to others.

What I Think

- Where did the Holy Spirit come from?

- How can I know when He helps me?

- Where does He live?

What God Wants Me to Know

1. After Jesus rose from the dead, He returned to heaven. God the Father sent the Holy Spirit to earth to remind us of all the things Jesus taught and to teach us many other things.

2. The Holy Spirit is God's gift to us. When we trust Jesus Christ to forgive our sins and be our Savior, the Holy Spirit comes to live inside us. He assures us that we belong to God.

3. The Holy Spirit is our helper and comforter. He prays for us, He protects us, and He gives us peace.

4. The Holy Spirit gives us power to do the right thing when we are tempted to do the wrong thing. He will help us control our desires and emotions. We make Him sad when we disobey God's rules.

5. We know the Holy Spirit is helping us when we can be kind and forgiving to others even when we don't feel like it.

6. We can ask the Holy Spirit to fill us with His strength and to let the fruit of the Spirit grow in our lives.

Look at It This Way...

Jesus said that the Holy Spirit is like wind—we can't see Him, but we can see what He does. We can't control the wind either. It blows where it wants to, and we aren't always sure what direction it will come from. The Holy Spirit's work is a mystery, but it is very real, and we benefit from His work in our lives. We know that the Spirit lives in everybody who believes in Jesus. The Spirit is with us to help us and to be our companion.

Prayer

Dear God,

Thank You for sending the Holy Spirit to be my helper and comforter. I want to please Him and make Him happy. Please fill me with His strength so I can have love, joy, peace, forbearance, kindness, goodness, faithfulness, gentleness, and self-control. Amen.

The Bible

Psalm 119:11,89,105
I have hidden your word in my heart
that I might not sin against You...
Your word, Lord, is eternal;
it stands firm in the heavens...
Your word is a lamp for my feet,
a light on my path.

2 Timothy 3:16-17
All Scripture is God-breathed and is useful for
teaching, rebuking, correcting and training in righteousness, so that the servant of God may be thor-
oughly equipped for every good work.

Hebrews 4:12
The word of God is alive and active. Sharper than
any double-edged sword, it penetrates even to
dividing soul and spirit, joints and marrow; it
judges the thoughts and attitudes of the heart.

The Bible is also called God's Word or Scripture. A long time ago God wanted to tell us many important things about Himself, things about the world, and things about ourselves—the people He created. He chose certain people to write down His words into books, and bit by bit, those books were put together into the one big book that we call the Bible.

What I Think

- Who are the people God spoke His words to?

- Does God speak to people today?

- The Bible was written a long time ago—why is it important to me now?

- I want to know what God thinks, but the Bible has big words and I don't think I could understand it.

What God Wants Me to Know

1. God gave us the Bible because He loved us and wants us to know about Him.

2. The Bible tells us that all Scripture came from God. It is very important for us to read it and understand what it is telling us.

3. God the Holy Spirit told certain people to write down what He said, including the words of Jesus. The Bible is complete—no one can add to it now.

4. The Bible has two parts—the Old Testament and the New Testament. The Old Testament tells us about the beginning of the world and God's chosen people (Israel). The New Testament tells us about Jesus Christ and how He wants us to live for Him.

5. The Bible trains us, corrects us, and teaches us how to live and be happy.

6. The Bible understands our thoughts and attitudes, and it helps us obey God. It gives us instructions on how to live.

7. Memorizing Scripture—storing God's Word in our minds and hearts—will help us live the way God wants us to.

8. God is always with us when we read the Bible because He is the author.

Look at It This Way...

One day a man bought a present for his wife—a beautiful jewelry box that glowed in the dark. His wife loved the gift, but when she put it in a darkened room, it didn't glow. Then the man and his wife found some instructions inside the box that said, "Put the box in the sunshine all day, and it will glow in the dark." They set the jewelry box beside a window for several hours, and sure enough, after the sun went down, the jewelry box glowed all night long.

Memorizing Scripture is similar to soaking up God's sunlight. If you hide His Word in your heart and mind, it will help you all day long to be happy and obedient. You will also be kind and helpful to others and tell them about God's love.

Prayer

Dear God,

Thank You for giving us the Bible. I know it is a very important book. It will teach me who You are and who I am. Help me to want to read it, love it, and obey it. Amen.

The Devil and the Armor of God

1 Peter 5:8-9

Be alert and of a sober mind. Your enemy the devil prowls around like a roaring lion looking for someone to devour. Resist him, standing firm in the faith.

Ephesians 6:10-13

Be strong in the Lord and in His mighty power. Put on the full armor of God, so that you can take your stand against the devil's schemes. For our struggle is not against flesh and blood, but against the rulers, against the authorities, against the powers of this dark world and against the spiritual forces of evil in the heavenly realms.

James 4:7

Submit yourselves, then, to God. Resist the devil, and he will flee from you.

The devil is also called Satan. He is God's enemy and our enemy. He is a spirit being that God allows to do bad things. The devil tells us lies and tries to trick us into disobeying God, but we don't have to be afraid of him. Instead, we can ask God to protect our minds and bodies, and we can put on His special armor.

What I Think

- Why is the devil (Satan) evil?
- How can something I can't see hurt me?
- Can the devil hurt me or make me do bad things?
- How do I put on and wear God's armor?
- How do I resist the devil?

What God Wants Me to Know

1. A long time ago, God created Satan as a beautiful angel to worship and serve Him in heaven. But Satan became evil and rebelled against God by trying to take His place.

2. So God sent Satan away, and Satan persuaded many other angels to go with him. They are called demons. Now Satan hates God and fights against Him.

3. Satan tricked Adam and Eve, the first man and woman, into disobeying God's rules. From that time on, every person has done bad things as well as good things.

4. God is much stronger than Satan and the invisible forces of evil. In fact, the devil knows that someday God will punish him forever and not allow him to do any more evil.

5. But right now, Satan tries to keep us from doing what God says. We can resist the devil by saying no to his plots against us.

6. God has given us special spiritual armor that will protect us from the devil's power. It includes the belt of truth, the vest of righteousness, the shoes of the gospel, the shield of faith, the

helmet of salvation, and the sword of the Spirit, which is the Word of God.

7. We can ask God to put His special armor on us whenever we need Him to.

Look at It This Way...

When soldiers fight in a war, they wear special clothes, a bulletproof vest, and a helmet. They carry a gun and other items that help protect them from the enemy.

The Bible tells us that we are fighting a war against evil forces we can't see. We can ask God to protect our minds and bodies, and we can cooperate with Him by putting on His special armor. The only part of the armor we can see is the sword of the Spirit, which is God's Word—the Bible.

In ancient times, when an army marched into battle, the soldiers linked their shields together, forming a long wall as they moved toward the enemy. This provided a way for the stronger soldiers to help the weaker ones. Also, it kept the enemy from breaking through their line of defense.

We cannot fight the devil on our own. We need the help of our family, our friends, and the people in our church. We can encourage and help each other by studying God's Word together, worshipping God together, and praying for each other.

Think of someone you can pray for right now so that both of you can become stronger in your faith—the shield that protects us from the attacks of the devil.

Prayer

Dear God,

I'm glad the devil is under Your power. I want to wear Your special armor every day so I'll be safe from him. Help me to memorize Scripture verses because they will protect me from the devil. My sword is the Word of God. Amen.

Angels

Psalm 103:21
Praise the LORD, all his heavenly hosts, you his servants who do his will.

Hebrews 1:14
Are not all angels ministering spirits sent to serve those who will inherit salvation?

Hebrews 13:2
Do not forget to show hospitality to strangers, for by so doing some people have shown hospitality to angels without knowing it.

God created angels to serve and worship Him and also to help us. Even though we cannot see them or feel them, they are real and are around us all the time. God gives them different jobs to do, and He assigns certain angels to protect us and to help us.

What I Think

- If angels are protecting me, why can't I see them?

- Do I have a guardian angel?

- How do I know if an angel helped me?

- Someday when I'm in heaven with Jesus, will I see the angels?

What God Wants Me to Know

1. Long ago God created millions of angels. They serve God, worshipping Him and doing whatever He tells them. They stay in God's presence unless He sends them out on a mission.

2. Angels don't have bodies like ours, but they can appear as people when God has an assignment for them to do. Sometimes God sends an angel to help someone who is in a dangerous or difficult situation. We usually don't know when an angel helps us.

3. Angels have various responsibilities. Only two are named in the Bible—Michael, who is always referred to as a leader among the angels, and Gabriel, who was sent by God to deliver messages. Gabriel is the one who told Mary she would be the mother of Jesus, the Messiah.

4. Angels love to see what God is doing on the earth. They were amazed that Jesus was willing to come to earth and save us from our sins. They pay particular attention to those who are God's children.

5. Angels spend much of their time worshipping God, and they celebrate when people accept Jesus Christ as their Savior.

Look at It This Way...

The Bible tells us about a man named Abraham who lived many years ago. One day, three visitors came to tell him an important message. He invited them to have a meal with him and his wife, Sarah. Later he discovered they were angels sent by God to warn him and his family that God was going to punish some wicked people who lived in a city near him. This true story shows that angels can appear as men even though they usually are invisible to us.

We should not expect to see angels even though they are constantly helping us. We can thank God that the angels obey Him and help us.

Prayer

Dear God,

Thank You for watching over me all the time. And thank You for sometimes sending an angel to protect me or help me. Amen.

The Ten Commandments

Deuteronomy 6:6-7

These commandments that I give you today are to be on your hearts. Impress them on your children. Talk about them when you sit at home and when you walk along the road, when you lie down and when you get up.

Psalm 19:7,9,11

The law of the LORD is perfect, refreshing the soul...The decrees of the LORD are firm, and all of them are righteous...In keeping them there is great reward.

John 1:17

The law was given through Moses; grace and truth came through Jesus Christ.

God gave us a set of laws called the Ten Commandments so that we would know right from wrong. If God tells us to do something and we don't do it, we are not keeping His commandments. And if God tells us *not* to do something and we do it anyway, we aren't keeping His commandments then either. These laws teach us about God and about ourselves. When we disobey God's laws, bad and hurtful things can happen to us and others. But when we obey God's laws, we can be happy and receive rewards and blessings from God.

What I Think

- Does God expect all people, even those who belong to other religions, to live by His laws?

- Should we try to keep all the laws today, or are some of them out of date?

- Should people make laws too, or should God be the only one who makes laws?

What God Wants Me to Know

1. The Ten Commandments are recorded in Exodus 20. The first law is the most important: "You shall have no other gods before me." This means that nothing should be as important to us as God. Jesus repeated this law by saying, "Love the Lord your God with all your heart and with all your soul and with all your mind."

2. These laws are basic and apply to people of every religion.

3. The tenth commandment—"You shall not covet"—shows us that God wants us to think correctly as well as live correctly. To covet is to want what someone else has. God says that desire is sinful.

4. No one but Jesus can keep all the commandments perfectly. God's laws remind us that we need God's forgiveness and grace.

5. The fifth commandment is very important. It says, "Honor

your father and your mother, so that you may live long in the land the LORD your God is giving you." To honor our parents is to respectfully obey them.

6. It is not wrong for people to make up their own laws as long as these laws are in agreement with God's laws.

Look at It This Way...

If you broke a cheap dish and had to pay for it, you wouldn't lose much money. But suppose you played with an expensive  china figurine that your parents told you not to touch. If it broke, you'd be in big trouble, and you would have to pay much more. Now suppose you were visiting the president at the White House, and while you were admiring a beautiful vase that once belonged to Abraham Lincoln, you accidently knocked it off the shelf. You might have to work for the rest of your life to earn enough money to pay for it.

When we break God's law, we are breaking something even more special. The cost of breaking God's laws is far more than anyone can ever pay. Thankfully, Jesus came to the earth to forgive us and to pay what we owe. He kept the law perfectly and then died for us so that God can honestly say that our debt is paid.

Prayer

Dear God,

I don't understand everything about Your laws, but I know that You gave them to us for our good and our protection. If I obey them, I will be safe and happy, and You will reward me. I want to respect and please You by keeping Your laws. Amen.

Sin

Romans 3:23
All have sinned and fall short of the glory of God.

Romans 6:12,23
Do not let sin reign in your mortal body so that you obey its evil desires...The wages of sin is death, but the gift of God is eternal life in Christ Jesus our Lord.

To sin is to disobey God's rules. To sin is to do things that displease God and that can hurt you and others, such as telling a lie, taking something that belongs to someone else, disobeying your parents, swearing, or hurting someone with your words or actions.

What I Think

- Sometimes I do or say things I don't really want to, but I can't stop myself.

- When other people take my things without asking, I get angry and want to hurt them.

- Some kids at school told a lie about me, and now I want to do something mean to them.

- Sometimes I do things my parents have told me not to do, and I feel bad afterward.

What God Wants Me to Know

1. The Bible tells us that everyone has sinned. Here is the reason why. Adam and Eve were innocent when God created them and put them in the beautiful Garden of Eden. God told them they could eat of every tree in the garden except one—the tree of the knowledge of good and evil.

2. The devil came to them in the form of a snake and told Adam and Eve a lie about God's words. He tricked them into thinking that God didn't love them. Both of them sinned by disobeying God and eating from the forbidden tree. Adam and Eve were ashamed and embarrassed, and they hid from God.

3. From that day on, everyone has been born with a desire to sin. That makes everyone a sinner. Sin separates people from God. It makes us feel sad and guilty.

4. Even when we don't want to sin, sometimes we sin anyway.

It is part of being human. The Bible describes this as our "sin nature."

5. Jesus came to the earth to be born into the human family and to die on the cross to be our Savior and save us from our sins.

Look at It This Way...

One day a man was walking along a beautiful sandy beach, and as he looked back at his footprints, he was surprised to see how crooked his path was. "Just like my life," he thought. "Every step is crooked."

Hours later, when he walked back to where he was staying, he could find no trace of his footprints. The tide had come in and washed them away. The beautifully clean and moist sand reminded him that he did not have to let his past mistakes control his future. Our sinful mistakes are terrible, but God's grace is greater than our sins. As we receive His salvation, He covers our sins and gives us a new beginning.

Prayer

Dear God,

Now I understand why I sometimes say or do things that I don't really want to. It's because I have a sin nature. Help me to remember that sin is always bad for me and that it displeases You. I'm glad Jesus came to be my Savior. Amen.

The Savior

John 3:16-17
God so loved the world that he gave his one and
only Son, that whoever believes in him shall not
perish but have eternal life. For God did not send
his Son into the world to condemn the world, but
to save the world through him.

Acts 2:23-24
This man [Jesus] was handed over to you by God's
deliberate plan and foreknowledge; and you, with
the help of wicked men, put him to death by nailing him to the cross. But God raised him from
the dead, freeing him from the agony of death,
because it was impossible for death to keep
its hold on him.

Romans 5:8-9
God demonstrates his own love for us in this:
While we were still sinners, Christ died for us.
Since we have now been justified by his blood, how
much more shall we be saved from God's wrath
through him!

A savior rescues people who are in danger. We are all sinners, so we are all in danger of God's anger and punishment for our sins. Only a qualified savior can rescue us. Jesus is the only one who never sinned, so only He can be the Savior. He chose to take the punishment for our sins so we wouldn't have to. Jesus loved us so much that He was willing to suffer and die a cruel death on a cross for the human race. He is now able to forgive us and cleanse us from our sins.

What I Think

- I wish Jesus didn't have to die for me, but I'm glad He did.
- Why was Jesus nailed on a cross? Wasn't there an easier way for Him to die?
- What is eternal life?

What God Wants Me to Know

1. When Jesus lived on earth, He told many people He was God and had come down from heaven. He taught that everyone had sinned. He healed many people and even raised people from the dead. He was able to forgive sins and help people in many ways.

2. The religious leaders didn't believe He was God. They were jealous that so many people listened to Jesus and followed Him. They were unhappy when Jesus did miracles and helped people, so they killed Him by nailing Him to a cross.

3. Jesus died on a cross even though He was completely innocent of any sin or crime. He was the only perfect person who ever lived, and He didn't deserve to die.

4. Jesus really was God. He always told the truth. All God's power was available to Him, so He could have stopped the people from killing Him. But He chose to suffer and die for the human family. This is called the crucifixion.

5. All of us deserve to be punished for our sins. But Jesus loved us so much that He chose to die in our place. Now God can forgive our sins and give us eternal life, and we will live with Jesus in heaven forever after we die. We will never be separated from Him.

6. We are thankful for the cross. It is important, special, and precious to us. When Jesus died, His blood flowed out. Though this is sometimes difficult to understand, the shed blood of Jesus is actually what forgives and cleanses our sins.

Look at It This Way...

A cross was made of two pieces of wood that were joined together to form a *T*. Crucifixion was a cruel death. The cross was laid on the ground, and the person's hands and feet were nailed to the wood. Then the cross was raised up and lowered into a hole in the ground. When you see a cross around someone's neck or in a church, remember that Jesus suffered and died on a cross to be our Savior. It reminds us of God's great love for us.

Prayer

Dear God,

Even though people committed a terrible crime when they killed Jesus, He died on the cross because He wanted to. I'm sad that He had to suffer so much, but I know He did it because He loved us very much. Please forgive my sins and be my Savior. Amen.

Forgiveness

Ephesians 4:32
Be kind and compassionate to one another, forgiving each other, just as in Christ God forgave you.

Colossians 3:13
Bear with each other and forgive one another if any of you has a grievance against someone. Forgive as the Lord forgave you.

When we forgive others, we choose not to hold their wrong against them any longer. We do not return evil for evil or try to get even. We accept the hurt and let them go free. That's what God did when He forgave us.

What I Think

- I feel bad when I disobey my mom or dad, but I always feel better when they forgive me.

- Sometimes forgiving people is difficult because I feel angry at them for what they did to me.

- If I forgive people, won't they get away with what they did? Won't they do it again?

What God Wants Me to Know

1. When we think about the way God has forgiven us, we become willing to forgive others.

2. ... for our forgiveness.

3. The decision to forgive someone does not mean that what the person did doesn't hurt us or that it is unimportant.

4. If someone is hurting you, tell your parents, a teacher, or someone else you trust right away. Never let anyone touch you inappropriately or force you to do something you know is wrong.

5. Forgiving others is not easy, but it makes us feel better inside and helps us to be kind to others.

Look at It This Way...

Once upon a time, a famous artist was deeply hurt by a friend. The artist, who was painting a picture of the Lord's Supper, decided to get even with his enemy by painting his face as the face of Judas, the man who betrayed Christ.

But when the artist attempted to paint the face of Jesus, he couldn't do it. He was frustrated because somehow he could not form the features of our Lord's face. Then the artist realized that his hatred toward his former friend was preventing him from painting the face of Jesus. Only when he repainted the face of Judas was he able to paint the face of Jesus.

In the same way, only when we forgive those who have hurt us are we able to be in complete fellowship with Jesus.

Prayer

Dear God,

Thank You for forgiving my sins. Sometimes I don't feel like forgiving, but help me to be like Jesus and forgive others just as You have forgiven me. Amen.

Redemption

Job 19:25
I know that my redeemer lives, and that in the end he will stand on the earth.

Ephesians 1:7-8
In him [Jesus] we have redemption through his blood, the forgiveness of sins, in accordance with the riches of God's grace that he lavished on us,

1 Peter 1:18-19
You know that it was not with perishable things such as silver or gold that you were redeemed from the empty way of life handed down to you from your ancestors, but with the precious blood of Christ, a lamb without blemish or defect.

In Bible times, people could *redeem* slaves. This means they could rescue slaves out of the slave market by paying whatever they were worth. Someone who paid the price was called a redeemer.

We are all sinners, so we need to be rescued from our desire to sin and from Satan, the master of sin. Jesus, our Redeemer, paid the price to free us from the slave market of sin. Now we can serve a new master—Jesus, the One who rescued us.

What I Think

- What price did Jesus have to pay to set me free from sin?
- Why couldn't Jesus pay the price with money?
- If I am redeemed, does that mean I won't sin anymore?

What God Wants Me to Know

1. Everyone is born into the slave market of sin. As sinners, we cannot pay for our own sin. God requires a payment that is impossible for us to make.

2. God could not accept money for our redemption. Jesus paid the complete price of redemption by dying on the cross and shedding His blood.

3. Jesus could pay our price and die in our place because He was part of the human family. God the Father could accept the payment Jesus made for us. The high price Jesus paid for us is proof that He loves us very much.

4. The blood of Jesus Christ is much more valuable than gold and silver. It is so precious and costly that God the Father accepted Jesus's death on the cross as a full payment for our sins. While He was dying on the cross, Jesus said, "Paid in full."

5. This is called redemption. It is the free gift of salvation from our sins. We don't have to work hard to earn it. All we have to do is accept it.

6. We have been bought by Jesus, so now we belong to Him. Being redeemed does not mean that we don't sin anymore, but it does mean that we do not have to give in to temptation. Now we are free to obey and serve Jesus Christ.

Look at It This Way...

A young boy once built a toy boat to float on a small lake near his house. He spent a lot of time putting it together, painting it, and testing it to make sure it could float.

One day a breeze blew the boat to the far side of the lake. He searched for it carefully but couldn't find it, and soon it became dark.

A week later he was walking along the street of his small town when he noticed his boat for sale in the window of a thrift shop. He went inside the shop and explained that the boat was his and that he had made it. But the store owner insisted that he had bought the boat from a man who had brought it to the store. The boy wanted it back so badly that he paid for it himself. Later he said, "The boat is mine twice—once because I made it, and a second time because I bought it."

We belong to God because He created us. But now we also belong to God in a special way because He redeemed us.

Prayer

Dear God,

Thank You for dying on the cross for me to redeem me from my sins. I accept Your free gift of salvation. You must love me very much. I want to obey and serve You. Amen.

Salvation

Romans 10:9-10

If you declare with your mouth, "Jesus is Lord," and believe in your heart that God raised him from the dead, you will be saved. For it is with your heart that you believe and are justified, and it is with your mouth that you profess your faith and are saved.

Ephesians 2:8-9 ESV

By grace you have been saved through faith. And this is not your own doing; it is the gift of God, not a result of works, so that no one may boast.

1 John 5:11-13

God has given us eternal life, and this life is in his Son. Whoever has the Son has life; whoever does not have the Son of God does not have life. I write these things to you who believe in the name of the Son of God so that you may know that you have eternal life.

Salvation is God's gift to us of Jesus's death on the cross to save us from our sins. We can be sure that Jesus has forgiven our sins and that we have eternal life and will belong to Him forever. That means we believe only in the death of Jesus—nothing else—for our salvation. Then we can know for sure that God has accepted us.

What I Think

- Why did Jesus die on the cross?
- How can I know that Jesus died for *me*?
- How many times do I need to ask Jesus to be my Savior?
- When I disobey, is Jesus still my Savior?
- If I haven't confessed all my sins, will I still go to heaven?

What God Wants Me to Know

1. The Bible tells us that everyone has disobeyed God in many ways. This disobedience is called sin, and sin keeps us away from God. Someday everyone must die for their sin.

2. God loved us so much that He sent His Son Jesus to the earth to die in our place.

3. Whoever accepts Jesus's death on the cross will be forgiven and have eternal life.

4. When Jesus becomes our Savior, God the Holy Spirit comes to live within us, helping us to know for sure that we are God's sons and daughters.

5. You only need to ask Jesus to be your Savior one time.

6. Even when we disobey God's rules, Jesus will always be our Savior, and no one can ever take that away from us. That is called *assurance of salvation*.

7. After we accept Jesus as our Savior, we know that we belong

to Him, but we still have to confess our sins to Him when we disobey.

Look at It This Way...

My husband and I have three daughters. When they disobeyed us or did something bad, we had to discipline them, and they had to ask our forgiveness for what they had done. But even when they disobeyed us, they were still our daughters, and we loved them just as much when they were bad as we did when they were good.

In the same way, when we accept Jesus as our Savior, we become members of His family and belong to Him forever. We only have to accept Him once, but we always have to confess our sins to Him when we disobey. We have assurance of salvation—we know that Jesus has received us into His family—and now that we belong to Him, we want to obey Him. When we mess up, we confess our mistakes and sins, and He forgives us.

Prayer

Dear God,

Thank You for loving me enough to send Jesus to earth to die for me. I accept Jesus's death on the cross for my sins. I am so glad that I can know for sure that Jesus is my Savior and that I belong to Your family. Amen.

Justification

Romans 5:1-2

Since we have been justified through faith, we have peace with God through our Lord Jesus Christ, through whom we have gained access by faith into this grace in which we now stand. And we boast in the hope of the glory of God.

Romans 8:33-34

Who will bring any charge against those whom God has chosen? It is God who justifies. Who then is the one who condemns? No one. Christ Jesus who died—more than that, who was raised to life—is at the right hand of God and is also interceding for us.

To be *justified* means that God considers us to be as good as Jesus. God sees us as if we had never sinned. When Jesus died in our place on the cross, He took our sins and gave us His righteousness (His goodness).

What I Think

- What if I do what I want to do instead of what Jesus wants me to do? Will God still accept me?

- If God considers me to be as good as Jesus, why do I still disobey?

- If I'm as good as Jesus, can I still do fun things?

What God Wants Me to Know

1. God can consider us to be as good as Jesus because Jesus died in our place. He took the punishment we deserved for our sin.

2. When we die, God will welcome us into heaven just as He welcomed Jesus Himself because we are accepted in Him.

3. Once we have received Jesus as our Savior, God will never change His mind about us. He will always love us, and we will always belong to Him.

4. We will still do bad things sometimes and make mistakes because we have a sin nature, just like everyone else. But that does not mean that sin is okay.

5. Whenever we know we've done something wrong, we must confess our sin to God and thank Him for forgiving us.

6. God is not angry with us. Even when we disobey and disappoint Him, He is always waiting for us to talk to Him. Jesus's death on the cross gives us peace with Him.

Look at It This Way...

A man was speeding along a stretch of highway when he was pulled over by a policeman. The man was given a ticket and had

to appear before a judge in court. The judge told the man he had to pay a fine of $100. The man didn't know what to do—he didn't have enough money to pay the fine. He was embarrassed and wondered what would happen to him.

But the judge was merciful. He rose from behind his desk, took off his big black robe, and stood beside the man. Then he took $100 from his own pocket and paid the fine for the poor man. The judge then returned to his desk and said to the man, "Your fine has been paid. You may go."

In the same way, we could not pay our debt to God, but Jesus, the righteous Judge, paid our debt so that we do not owe God anything. God now sees us as if we'd never sinned. He proclaims that we are considered as good as Jesus, and He tells us that we are free to serve Him with joy.

Prayer

Dear God,

I can hardly believe that You think I'm as good as Jesus! But Jesus died in my place and paid my sin debt, so I will believe what the Bible says about me. Please help me to love You with all my heart and live for You. Amen.

Obedience

Proverbs 20:11 NLT
Even children are known by the way they act, whether their conduct is pure, and whether it is right.

Ephesians 6:1-3
Children, obey your parents in the Lord, for this is right. "Honor your father and mother"—which is the first commandment with a promise—"that it may go well with you and that you may enjoy long life on the earth."

To obey is to do the right thing even when you want to do the wrong thing. God can help you do what is right even when someone else wants you to do something that is wrong. You will be happy and successful when you choose to obey your parents and God's rules, which are found in the Bible.

What I Think

I need courage to obey by doing the right thing...

- when a friend invites me to watch a bad movie
- when I feel like telling a lie
- when I am tempted to take something that doesn't belong to me
- when I want to get even with my brother or sister who took something of mine
- when I want to do something that my parents have told me not to do

What God Wants Me to Know

1. The Bible says that obeying God and our parents is the right thing to do and that it pleases God.

2. God gave us wise parents who can teach us what is right and wrong.

3. If we do not obey our parents and teachers, we will not learn how to obey God.

4. When we obey, we are more likely to be happy and peaceful.

5. Sometimes we choose not to obey, and then we often feel sad and angry. When that happens, we can pray to God, asking Him to forgive us and to help us obey next time. Then we should tell our parents that what we did was wrong and ask them to forgive us.

6. We should talk to a parent, a teacher, or someone else we trust when it is hard to obey. They will not make fun of us, because

they love us and want to help us. Even though obedience may not be easy, it is always the best choice.

Look at It This Way...

A man who was looking for work walked into the office of a well-known businessman. The businessman told him, "If you want to work here, I'll show you a pile of bricks you can carry to the other side of the yard and stack."

The man worked hard all day long. When he was finished and paid for his work, he asked if he could return to work the next day. The businessman said, "Sure. Come back tomorrow and carry the bricks back to where you found them this morning." The man returned and did exactly as the employer requested. The next day the man received the same instructions. For a full week, he did nothing but carry the bricks back and forth each day, stacking them neatly.

So the man was hired to go to stores and buy the goods his employer requested. The businessman said, "I tested him, and know I can trust him to obey."

Just as the man obeyed his employer, we must obey even when we don't understand all the reasons why we have to do some things. Obedience in small things is a test for greater responsibility.

Prayer

Dear God,

Sometimes it's hard for me to be good and to obey. Please give me the courage to do the right thing. Thank You for my parents, who love me. I know that obeying them makes them happy, it makes You happy, and eventually, it will make me happy too. Amen.

Discipline

Job 5:17
Blessed is the one whom God corrects; so do not despise the discipline of the Almighty.

Hebrews 12:5-7,11
"My son [or daughter], do not make light of the Lord's discipline, and do not lose heart when he rebukes you, because the Lord disciplines the one he loves, and he chastens everyone he accepts as his son [or daughter]." Endure hardship as discipline. God is treating you as his children. For what children are not disciplined by their father?...No discipline seems pleasant at the time, but painful. Later on, however, it produces a harvest of righteousness and peace for those who have been trained by it.

To be disciplined is to be corrected for disobeying rules. Just as children are disciplined by their parents, God our heavenly Father disciplines us, His children. Everyone who is part of God's family—every son and every daughter—needs to be corrected. Discipline trains us to want to do what is right.

What I Think

- Sometimes I think my parents are too strict and discipline me too much.

- My parents discipline me by taking away one of my favorite activities.

- How does God discipline us?

What God Wants Me to Know

1. Discipline helps us understand that God doesn't like sin. It helps us remember to obey His rules.

2. God disciplines us because He loves us. He does it for our good.

3. Discipline teaches us things we wouldn't learn if we got away with doing wrong things. It trains us to do what is right.

4. Sometimes God's discipline may hurt, but He wants us to become obedient. He wants us to stay away from things that will harm us.

5. God disciplines us by letting us experience the consequences of breaking His rules or the rules our parents have given us.

6. When we do bad things in secret, God often lets other people find out because sin turns our hearts away from Him. He loves us too much to let us get away with sin. The Bible says in Numbers 32:23, "You may be sure that your sin will find you out."

Look at It This Way...

Todd and his friends were walking home from school one day when they decided to sneak into a neighbor's garden and take some of the produce. The leader of the group even talked them into pulling out some of the corn and tomatoes. When a neighbor saw them making a mess of the garden, he scolded the children and called their parents. Todd's father came over immediately to see what was happening.

When Todd's father arrived, he said nothing to all the other children but walked directly to Todd, taking him by the arm and leading him home to discipline him. That day Todd learned the mean-

ing of the word *discipline* by experiencing it firsthand! But why did Todd's father not discipline the other children? The reason is that the other children were not his. Todd was his son, and that is what made the difference. In the same way, our heavenly Father is faithful to discipline His own sons and daughters.

Prayer

Dear God,

I know that sometimes I need to be disciplined by You and by my parents. Help me to accept discipline even though it may hurt. I know that You love me and that You discipline me for my good. I want to be trained to obey. Amen.

Conscience

Hebrews 9:14
How much more, then, will the blood of Christ, who through the eternal Spirit offered himself unblemished to God, cleanse our consciences from acts that lead to death, so that we may serve the living God!

Hebrews 10:22
Let us draw near to God with a sincere heart and with the full assurance that faith brings, having our hearts sprinkled to cleanse us from a guilty conscience and having our bodies washed with pure water.

1 John 1:9 ESV
If we confess our sins, he is faithful and just to forgive us our sins and to cleanse us from all unrighteousness.

1 John 3:20-21
If our hearts condemn us, we know that God is greater than our hearts, and he knows everything.

Everyone has a conscience. It is our inner sense of right and wrong—we sometimes refer to it as our heart. It reminds us that the things we do or think are right or wrong. Our conscience can make us feel good and happy or guilty and sad.

What I Think

- Sometimes I think I'm a bad person.
- I don't know what to do when I feel guilty.
- Some of my friends do bad things but don't seem to feel guilty.
- How can I have a clear conscience?

What God Wants Me to Know

1. God gave you a conscience so that you would be reminded that some things are right and some things are wrong.

2. Your conscience is influenced by what you know. That is why it's very important to memorize God's Word—so you will know what God says is right and wrong.

3. Your conscience helps you choose to do what you know is right, and it makes you feel guilty when you ignore it and do what you know is wrong.

4. As you learn more about God, your conscience will let you know when you have broken His laws.

5. Guilt is the knowledge that you have disobeyed God's rules, your parents' rules, or any other laws that have been put in place to keep the world in order.

6. A guilty conscience will remind you to confess your sin and ask God to cleanse you. The Bible says that God is faithful to do this.

7. When you disobey your parents or teacher, or when you hurt someone by your words or actions, it is very important that you ask them to forgive you.

8. Some people have broken God's rules so many times, their

consciences don't work very well, so they don't feel very much guilt anymore.

Look at It This Way...

When you trip and fall into a mud puddle, you can get cleaned up, and your clothes can be washed. But what do you do when you feel dirty inside—down deep where no soap can reach? Thankfully, Jesus is willing and able to forgive your sin and "cleanse you from all unrighteousness." That means that God not only takes our sin away but also gives us the assurance that we have been cleaned up inside.

To confess our sins is to agree with God about what our conscience tells us and what God's Word tells us. We admit that (1) we have sinned, and we must name the sin to God, and that (2) Jesus is able to forgive every confessed sin, no matter what it is. Then we accept His cleansing.

After confessing our sin, if we still feel dirty inside, we must insist that God's Word is true by thanking Him that we have been forgiven. David, a king in the Old Testament whose conscience troubled him because of a sin he had committed, prayed that God would wash him "whiter than snow." What God did for him, God does for us—thanks to Jesus.

Prayer

Dear God,

I'm so glad that Jesus will forgive my sin and cleanse me. I want to be close to God, and I want to have a clean heart. I feel much better when I know I have been forgiven. Amen.

Temptation

1 Corinthians 10:13
No temptation has overtaken you except what is common to mankind. And God is faithful; he will not let you be tempted beyond what you can bear. But when you are tempted, he will also provide a way out so that you can endure it.

James 1:13-14
When tempted, no one should say, "God is tempting me." For God cannot be tempted by evil, nor does he tempt anyone; but each person is tempted when they are dragged away by their own evil desire and enticed.

Temptation is an invitation or a desire to do something that we know is wrong or that would disobey the rules of God and others in authority over us. Temptation comes to us in many ways. We are tempted to give in to the way we feel, what we see, what we want to have, and what we want to do. The good news is that we don't have to give in to these desires. God can help us say no.

What I Think

- Why is it so easy to give in to temptation?
- Why is it so hard to say no?
- How do I say no when I really want to do something wrong?
- Is everyone tempted to do bad things or only some people?

What God Wants You to Know

1. Sometimes we will feel like doing something bad, such as telling a lie, cheating in school, taking something that is not ours, looking at something that is harmful to our minds and hearts, or hurting someone with our words or actions.

2. The Bible says that our enemy, the devil, prowls around like a roaring lion looking for someone to devour. That means the devil wants us to give in to temptation and sin, and to get in trouble. He deceives us into thinking that sin is fun and won't hurt anyone.

3. No matter what temptation we face, others have already been in the same situation we are in. They have found the strength and courage—also called moral fortitude—to say no to temptation and to do what is right.

4. We can say no and resist temptation in three ways. First, we can be alert and have sober minds. That means we should be serious and think about the consequences of our choices and actions.

5. Second, we can prepare to face temptation by deciding ahead of time that we will not give in. This is part of having good

character—doing what is right when no one is watching. Quoting Bible verses we have memorized strengthens our decision to say no.

6. Third, through prayer, we can depend on Jesus—our Savior from sin—to help us. He is always with us by the power of the Holy Spirit. We belong to Jesus, and He is waiting for us to ask Him to help us.

Look at It This Way...

A man described his inner struggles this way: "It is as though I have two dogs fighting inside me. One dog wants me to do what is good, and the other dog wants me to do what is bad."

"Which one wins?" someone asked him.

"The one I feed the most!" he answered.

That explains why we must spend time feeding what is good inside us by memorizing Scripture, studying the Bible, praying, going to church, and choosing friends with good character. All of these things help us say no to temptation.

Prayer

Dear Jesus,

Thank You for always being with me in every temptation I face. Please give me the moral strength to say no when I am tempted to disobey. I want to have good character and set an example for others to follow. Amen.

Guarding Your Mind

Psalm 19:14 ESV
Let the words of my mouth and the meditation of my heart be acceptable in your sight, O Lord, my rock and my redeemer.

Romans 12:2
Do not conform to the pattern of this world, but be transformed by the renewing of your mind. Then you will be able to test and approve what God's will is—his good, pleasing and perfect will.

Philippians 4:8
Brothers and sisters, whatever is true, whatever is noble, whatever is right, whatever is pure, whatever is lovely, whatever is admirable—if anything is excellent or praiseworthy—think about such things.

Our minds and hearts are deep inside us. They are where we think, feel, and make decisions. The things we see and hear influence our minds and thoughts. If we watch and listen to people swearing and doing bad things on TV, we will be influenced to do the same things. If we choose friends who behave badly, we'll feel pressured to do the same. We guard our minds and thoughts by protecting them from evil words, pictures, people, and activities. We choose friends and things that are excellent and worthy of praise.

What I Think

- How can I control what I see and hear?

- What should I do when my family or friends watch a bad show on TV?

- Sometimes I have scary or bad thoughts and I don't know how to get rid of them.

What God Wants Me to Know

1. Guarding your heart, mind, and thoughts is one of the most important things you can do. It is more important than putting a lock on your locker at school to protect your valuable belongings.

2. Your mind and heart are influenced by the things you see on TV, the games you play, the books and magazines you read, and the things you hear.

3. The thoughts you store in your mind and heart will eventually come out in the things you say and do, whether they are selfish and angry or loving and respectful.

4. After you trust Jesus as your Savior, God makes a change in your heart and mind. You begin to love God and want to please Him. You also begin to love others more than yourself, and you want to be kind and helpful.

5. The Bible teaches that you must not think like someone who does not know God and His rules. You can renew your mind by memorizing Scripture and studying God's Word. You can also turn away from worthless things and bad thoughts, focus your mind on pure and lovely things, and ask God to protect you by putting His special armor on your mind and body.

Look at It This Way...

In ancient times, castles were built with strong, heavy doors to keep out enemies. Before people could enter, they had to identify themselves as friends or enemies. Our minds are like castles with strong doors that are locked on the inside. When bad or scary thoughts try to enter, we must keep the doors locked and protect our minds and thoughts from being invaded by the enemy.

Prayer

Dear God,

Let the words of my mouth and the meditation of my heart be acceptable in Your sight. Amen.

Anger

Proverbs 22:24-25
Do not make friends with a hot-tempered person,
do not associate with one easily angered, or you
may learn their ways and get yourself ensnared.

Proverbs 29:22
An angry person stirs up conflict, and a hot-
tempered person commits many sins.

Ephesians 4:26-27
"In your anger do not sin": Do not let the sun go
down while you are still angry, and do not give the
devil a foothold.

James 1:19-20
Everyone should be quick to listen, slow to speak
and slow to become angry, because human anger
does not produce the righteousness that
God desires.

Anger is a normal human emotion. Sometimes we get angry when our rights are overlooked or we don't get our way. Some anger is good, and some anger is bad. We feel good anger when we see something that is wrong and that hurts others. We feel bad anger when we overreact to something or want to hurt someone. God warns us that anger can lead to doing sinful things that will hurt us and others.

What I Think

- I have a right to be angry when I'm mistreated.
- When I'm angry, I want to get even.
- I get angry more easily on some days than on others.
- Some things make me angry every time they happen.
- It scares me when I get really angry.

What God Wants Me to Know

1. We should be angry about some things, such as injustice, abuse, mistreatment, and cruelty. We also feel angry when our rights are overlooked, when we are cheated out of what should be ours, when we are unfairly punished, or when we are falsely accused, made fun of, disrespected, or humiliated.

2. Angry outbursts and uncontrolled anger can cause us to hurt others with our words and actions. An angry person can cause trouble and disturb the peace.

3. We can learn to control our anger by...
   a. admitting we are angry and making a decision to control our anger
   b. confessing any sin to God that is making us feel angry, guilty, and defensive
   c. resisting our enemy, the devil, by praying, memorizing Bible verses, and putting on the armor of God
   d. talking to our parents, grandparents, or teachers about how we feel

4. When we feel ourselves becoming angry, we can...

   a. say a quick prayer to God to help us stay in control

   b. count to ten and stay calm

   c. think before we speak hurtful words or act out our anger by hitting someone

   d. remember that God wants us to treat others with patience and love—just as He treats us

Look at It This Way...

A Sunday school teacher placed a big target on a wall and invited his students to draw a picture of someone who made them angry and pin it on the target. One girl drew a picture of a

former friend who had told a lie about her. A boy drew a picture of a kid who had bullied and made fun of him. When the target was full of pictures, all the students threw darts at them.

After a few minutes the teacher interrupted them. He removed the pictures and the front of the target. Underneath was a picture of Jesus. Holes and jagged marks covered His face, and His eyes were pierced out. No words were necessary. That day the students learned that every angry dart thrown at those who have wronged them lands in the heart of Jesus.

Prayer

Dear God,

I don't like to feel angry and say or do things that hurt others. Please help me to learn how to control my anger. I want to show love and kindness to others even when I don't think they deserve it. Amen.

Discernment

Proverbs 2:10-11
Wisdom will enter your heart, and knowledge will be pleasant to your soul. Discretion will protect you, and understanding will guard you.

Proverbs 3:5-6
Trust in the LORD with all your heart and lean not on your own understanding; in all your ways submit to him, and he will make your paths straight.

Proverbs 15:14
The discerning heart seeks knowledge, but the mouth of a fool feeds on folly.

Discernment is the ability to tell the difference between right and wrong. Sometimes it is hard to tell the difference because some wrong things seem good, and some good things seem bad. Discernment involves three things: (1) trusting God's love and care for you with all your heart, (2) always depending on God's great knowledge and not your own, and (3) talking with God about what you want to do and obeying Him even when you don't want to.

What I Think

- Sometimes I feel confused as to what is right and wrong.

- If I look and act different from my friends, they might make fun of me.

- It's hard to do what I know is right when my friend wants me to something else.

- If I don't choose the right thing, am I a bad person?

What God Wants Me to Know

1. We make right choices by learning what God says is right and wrong.

2. Some people don't love God or the Bible, and they don't want to obey His rules. They may make up their own rules and even try to get others to do what is wrong.

3. God wants us to know the difference between good and bad movies, videos, games, books, magazines, and so on. Watching and reading bad ones can lead to sinful thoughts and actions.

4. God wants us to discern what is right by trusting Him more than we trust ourselves.

5. Ask God to help you always remember the most important goals in life—to know God, love Him, and please Him in everything you do.

Look at It This Way...

Candice was excited about her shopping trip with her mother. She loved finding new clothes for school. But after they had visited a few stores, Candice and her mother began to argue. Candice wanted to wear an outfit that would attract everyone's attention. She told her mother that it looked like the clothes her friends in school wear.

But her mother told her, "Candice, you are different from other girls. I want people to be attracted to you because of your kindness and who you are as a person and not because you wear flashy outfits."

Candice learned that discernment is important in all the decisions we make—what to wear, whom to be friends with, and where to go. God wants us to be different from those who aren't concerned about the instructions He gave us in the Bible.

Prayer

Dear God,

Thank You for the Bible, which tells me how to obey You. Sometimes, doing what is right is difficult, but I want to please You. I want to make wise choices and discern right from wrong. Please help me to know You, love You, and please You in everything I do. Amen.

Friendship

Psalm 1:1-2
Blessed is the one who does not walk in step with the wicked or stand in the way that sinners take or sit in the company of mockers, but whose delight is in the law of the LORD, and who meditates on his law day and night.

Proverbs 17:17
A friend loves at all times, and a brother is born for a time of adversity.

Proverbs 18:24
One who has unreliable friends soon comes to ruin, but there is a friend who sticks closer than a brother.

Friends are very important. God wants us to have friends so we can have fun and enjoy doing things together. The best friends are those who encourage us to do what is right and good. We influence our friends and they influence us—either in good ways or in bad ways. Some kids may be very friendly and nice when with a group, but when they are alone with you they may suggest that you do something that is wrong and that will hurt you. That's why we must be careful when choosing our friends.

What I Think

- Some kids who like me want to be my friends, but they say and do things I know are wrong.

- How do I say no to someone who is a bad influence but really wants to be my friend?

- My best friend is a nice person, but sometimes he or she swears or tells a lie.

- What is peer pressure?

- How can I make friends with other kids?

What God Wants Me to Know

1. A *peer* is a person who is like you, so when other kids try to get you to do something (or *pressure* you), you are feeling *peer pressure.*

2. Choose friends who will encourage you to do what is right and good. It is better to be alone than to be in bad company.

3. Don't have close friends who say bad words, make fun of others, watch bad things on TV or the Internet, disrespect their parents, or try to get you to disobey your parents.

4. Talk to your parents about your friends. Tell your parents or teacher if anyone threatens to hurt you if you don't do something they want you to do.

5. To have friends, you must be friendly and show kindness to others. This isn't easy for a shy person, but you can invite people to sit with you at lunchtime or offer to help them with a project or homework.

6. Remember that Jesus is your best friend. He is with you all the time!

Look at It This Way...

Helen Keller was blind and deaf—she couldn't see or hear. But her friend, Anne Sullivan, who herself was partially blind,

decided to spend her life helping the blind. In two weeks Anne taught Helen how to spell 30 words by tracing the letters on her hand. They worked together for many years and Helen eventually became a famous author and speaker.

When Anne became completely blind near the end of her life, Helen taught her much more about how to read braille. In all they were friends for 49 years! That is true friendship—one person helping another who has a need.

Prayer

Dear God,

Help me to choose my friends wisely. I want to be a good example and influence my friends to say and do good things. Please help me to say no to anyone who wants me to disobey You or my parents. Amen.

Character and Courage

Proverbs 3:5-6
Trust in the LORD with all your heart and lean not on your own understanding; in all your ways submit to him, and he will make your paths straight.

Proverbs 4:23
Above all else, guard your heart, for everything you do flows from it.

Joshua 1:9
Have I not commanded you? Be strong and courageous. Do not be afraid; do not be discouraged, for the LORD your God will be with you wherever you go.

1 Corinthians 16:13
Be on your guard; stand firm in the faith; be courageous; be strong.

Character is who we really are inside. It is our willingness and ability to do the right thing—to behave well not only when our parents, teachers, or friends can see us, but also when we are alone and no one is looking. Courage is doing the right thing even when we are tempted to do the wrong thing. To have courage is to stand up for what we know is right even when someone makes fun of what we believe. It is choosing to do the right thing even if our friends choose to do what we know is wrong.

What I Think

- When I don't obey, does that mean I have bad character?
- How do I develop good character?
- Sometimes I feel sad, angry, or guilty when I don't have the courage to make wise choices.
- I need courage to...
  - tell the truth when I feel like telling a lie
  - leave other people's things alone
  - treat my brother or sister kindly when they are mean to me or take my stuff
  - obey my parents when I don't want to
  - do what is right when my friends want me to do something I know is wrong

What God Wants Me to Know

1. The most important part of us is on the inside, where no one but God can see. The Bible calls this place the heart. It's where we think, feel, make decisions, and respond to other people.

2. People of good character have convictions—deeply held beliefs that help them make good decisions.

3. Our convictions should be based on God's teaching in the Bible. We should never go against our convictions. Neither

should we argue with others and try to force them to believe what we do.

4. Having the courage to follow our convictions will help others to understand what we believe.

5. People of good character always tell the truth—even when it hurts. But no one is perfect, and sometimes we tell a lie or say bad things about others to defend ourselves or make ourselves look better.

6. People with courage admit when they have lied, and they make things right. Doing this keeps us from having bad character.

7. Even when we sin and make mistakes, God still loves us. His forgiveness and grace are always there to help us when we fail.

Look at It This Way...

To develop my character and build up my courage, I can...

- memorize Bible verses that teach me right from wrong
- pray and ask God to give me courage to do the right thing
- listen to my parents, who are older and wiser than me
- talk to a parent, a teacher, or someone else I trust when anyone bullies or threatens me
- pick friends who love God and want to obey His rules

Prayer

Dear God,

I want to be a person of good character and have convictions that will guide me when I'm tempted to do something wrong. Give me the courage to stand up for what I believe even if someone makes fun of me. I know You are with me and will help me wherever I go. Amen.

The Fear of the Lord

Psalm 31:19

How abundant are the good things that you have stored up for those who fear you, that you bestow in the sight of all, on those who take refuge in you.

Psalm 111:10

The fear of the LORD is the beginning of wisdom; all who follow his precepts have good understanding. To him belongs eternal praise.

Proverbs 1:7

The fear of the LORD is the beginning of knowledge, but fools despise wisdom and instruction.

Proverbs 8:13

To fear the LORD is to hate evil.

God is the Lord. To fear the Lord is to show Him reverence by our worship, love, and obedience. God is holy and righteous and without sin. We must respect His rules and know that there are consequences for disobeying Him. Fearing the Lord makes us wise and gives us knowledge.

What I Think

- Should I be afraid of God?
- How can I learn to fear the Lord?
- How can I show God that I fear Him?
- How can I know what God wants me to do?
- I don't want to be a fool!

What God Wants Me to Know

1. When you fear God, you don't use His name to express surprise or anger, such as "Oh my God!" even if your friends do.

2. When you fear God, you resist the temptation to do what is wrong.

3. When you fear God, you ask yourself, "What would God want me to do in this situation?" Then you ask God for wisdom to make the right choice.

4. When you fear God, you obey your parents and teachers and treat them with respect. This helps you learn to respect God as well.

5. When you fear God, you aren't afraid of Him. Rather, you try to please Him in all you do.

6. When you fear God, you begin each day by asking Him to guide you and keep you from what is wrong.

7. When you fear God, you confess your sin to Him as soon as you are aware of it. He will forgive you and help you be more obedient next time.

Look at It This Way...

The Bible tells us a story from Moses's life. When the Israelites were in the desert, they became very thirsty, and they blamed Moses for leading them into the wilderness. God promised Moses that if he spoke to a certain rock, water would flow and the people would be able to drink.

Moses was angry at the people because they had been complaining, so instead of speaking to the rock, he hit it with his

staff. Water flowed out, and the people were glad they could drink. But God told Moses that because he hit the rock instead of speaking to it, he would not be allowed to enter the special land God promised to give His people. God forgave Moses for his disobedience, but because he did not fear God enough to obey Him, he had to live with this disappointment.

The fear of the Lord motivates us to obey Him. When we disobey, God forgives us, but we too have to live with the consequences of our choices.

Prayer

Dear God,

I know You are holy, and I want to fear and respect You in the proper way. Your rules are hard to obey sometimes, but I want to please You in all I do. Please give me the desire to obey. And when I disobey, help me remember to confess my sin to You and ask for forgiveness. Amen.

Worry

Isaiah 41:10
Do not fear, for I am with you; do not be dismayed, for I am your God. I will strengthen you and help you; I will uphold you with my righteous right hand.

Matthew 6:34
Do not worry about tomorrow, for tomorrow will worry about itself. Each day has enough trouble of its own.

Philippians 4:6-7
Do not be anxious about anything, but in every situation, by prayer and petition, with thanksgiving, present your requests to God. And the peace of God, which transcends all understanding, will guard your hearts and your minds in Christ Jesus.

1 Peter 5:7
Cast all your anxiety on him because he cares for you.

To worry, or to have anxiety, is to think a lot about things that make us sad or things that we are afraid might happen. Worry takes away our energy, our desire to study, and our ability to sleep well and do other important things. Worrying about problems doesn't make them any better.

What I Think

I sometimes feel sad or afraid when...

- a boy or girl at school teases me or makes fun of me
- my dad or mom doesn't live with my family
- my pet is lost
- my grandma or grandpa is sick
- my family has to move to a different city
- my dad or mom doesn't have a job

What God Wants Me to Know

1. It's okay to feel sad or to cry when someone hurts you. But thinking about it a lot can make you feel even sadder or angrier.

2. Always talk to a parent, a teacher, or someone else you trust about anything that makes you afraid, sad, or worried.

3. The Bible teaches that we don't have to worry. Here's why:

   a. You are very important to God. He loves you and cares about you and all the things that happen to you.

   b. Worry will not change anything. Your thoughts and feelings cannot make your problem go away—but they might make your stomach hurt or give you a bad dream.

   c. God wants you to talk to Him about anything that makes you afraid, sad, or worried. Your problems may not change or go away, but He wants to help you and make your worry and fears go away. He wants to give you peace.

4. Peace is the opposite of worry.

Look at It This Way...

A famous baseball player was asked whether he worries. He replied, "I don't worry over things I can control, because I'm in charge of them. And I don't worry over things I can't control, because worry doesn't change anything. So I have made up my mind to not worry."

When asked how he kept worry out of his mind, he replied, "I focus on a promise from the Bible, and I don't let myself be drawn to worrisome thoughts. Worry and fear would like to take control over all my thoughts, but I don't let them."

Prayer

Dear God,

When I'm worried or sad about something, I will talk to You about it because I know that You care about me. Thank You for helping me when I am afraid. Please help me learn to trust You to help me with my problems. Thank You for putting peace in my mind and heart. Amen.

Grace

2 Corinthians 8:9
You know the grace of our Lord Jesus Christ, that though he was rich, yet for your sake he became poor, so that you through his poverty might become rich.

Ephesians 2:8-9
It is by grace you have been saved, through faith and this is not from yourselves, it is the gift of God—not by works, so that no one can boast.

Hebrews 4:16
Let us then approach God's throne of grace with confidence, so that we may receive mercy and find grace to help us in our time of need.

G race is God's kindness and favor, which we don't deserve because we are sinners. By His grace, God provided everything we need for our sins to be forgiven. When we receive salvation and become God's children, He takes care of us in many special ways. He saves us, forgives us, cleanses us, protects us, helps us, guides us, provides for us, and blesses us with many other spiritual blessings.

What I Think

- Do I have to do good things to receive God's grace?
- I don't deserve God's grace, so why does He give it to me?
- Is God's grace completely free, or is it only for those who try to be good?

What God Wants Me to Know

1. We can do some good things that please God, but we can't do enough good things to make us right with God.
2. God provides the only thing we need to be right with Him— Jesus's death on the cross to forgive our sins. Christ's death and resurrection make our salvation possible.
3. We receive salvation through God's grace. God makes us right with Him through Jesus.
4. We cannot earn our salvation. It is a free gift of God's grace.
5. By His grace, God also helps us please Him every day.
6. Grace helps us in many ways—when we're sad, worried, angry, or sick; when we need to solve a problem; and when we're hurt or misunderstood.
7. Grace is such a special gift from God, we can say it is *amazing*!

Look at It This Way...

A missionary who lived in India became good friends with an Indian pearl diver. The missionary often had conversations with his friend, trying to help the Hindu man understand that the salvation Jesus died to give us is a free gift. One day the Indian gave the missionary a large, beautiful, perfect pearl as a gift. The pearl

diver explained that his own son had lost his life diving for the pearl in the bottom of the sea.

The missionary thanked him but said, "I can't accept this for free. Let me pay you for this beautiful pearl."

The Indian replied, "This pearl cost my son his life. It is priceless—no amount of money could pay for it."

Then the truth dawned on the Indian. Our salvation cost Jesus His life. We cannot pay for what Jesus did for us. Nothing we could offer God is as valuable as the suffering and death of His beloved Son. We can't earn it or pay for it—that's why the gift of salvation is free.

Prayer

Dear God,

Thank You for Your grace, which comes to help me in my time of need. You are there for me anytime I call for help. I love You! Amen.

Giving Thanks

Psalm 100:3-5

Know that the LORD is God. It is he who made us, and we are his. We are his people, the sheep of his pasture. Enter his gates with thanksgiving and his courts with praise; give thanks to him and praise his name. For the LORD is good and his love endures forever; his faithfulness continues through all generations.

1 Thessalonians 5:18

Give thanks in all circumstances; for this is God's will for you in Christ Jesus.

Giving thanks to God for everything means that we develop an attitude of thankfulness in every situation, even during the hard times in our lives. The secret to being content is to give thanks.

What I Think

- Sometimes when I don't get what I want, I feel angry and upset.

- I think my parents treat my brother or sister better than they treat me, and that isn't fair.

- How can I be thankful when a kid at school is mean to me?

- How can I be thankful when my mom or dad won't let me do something I really want to do?

What God Wants Me to Know

1. We are to give thanks *in* all circumstances, not *for* all circumstances. You don't give thanks to God for what is bad or evil. Still, God can use those things for your good.

2. When you give thanks to God, you honor Him by reminding yourself that God is in charge of everything.

3. To become a more thankful person, make a list of all the things you are thankful for, and add to the list whenever you think of something new. Take time every week to thank God for these blessings in your life.

4. When you are upset or discouraged because you didn't get what you wanted, instead of complaining, whining, getting angry, or saying mean things, you can look at your list and see all the wonderful things you can be thankful for.

5. Giving thanks to God even when you are disappointed helps you to accept your situation. Amy Carmichael, a dedicated Christian woman who lived many years ago and was often sick, said these helpful words: "In acceptance there is peace."

Look at It This Way...

David Beamer was eight years old when his dad, whose name was Todd, died in an airplane crash on September 11, 2001. A few months later on Todd's birthday, David's mother, Lisa, was feeling especially sad because she missed her husband so much. When David asked his mother why she felt so sad, she said, "Because Daddy isn't with us on his birthday."

David replied, "But, Mom, we can still have cake, can't we?"

Even though many difficult things happen to us, we can always find a reason to give thanks to God. Even when we're sad or our plans don't work out, we can thank God for the many blessings He has given us—even for cake.

Prayer

Dear God,

Thank You for always listening when I need to talk to You. Help me to learn to thank You for the good things in my life even when I'm sad, angry, upset, or hurt. I know You will help me and work everything out for my good. Amen.

Death and Grief

Psalm 23:4 ESV
Even though I walk through the valley of the shadow of death, I will fear no evil, for you are with me; your rod and your staff, they comfort me.

Philippians 1:21
For to me, to live is Christ and to die is gain.

1 Thessalonians 4:13-14,18
Brothers and sisters, we do not want you to be uninformed about those who sleep in death, so that you do not grieve like the rest of mankind, who have no hope. For we believe that Jesus died and rose again, and so we believe that God will bring with Jesus those who have fallen asleep in him...Therefore encourage one another with these words.

Death is part of life because nothing on this earth can live forever. Everything and everyone dies at some time—plants, animals, and people. People can die at any age. Some people die when they are young, but most people die when they are old. No one knows when or how they will die. When someone we love dies, we cry and feel very sad because we will miss our loved one very much. We call this sadness grief.

What I Think

- What happens when we die?
- What happens to us after we die?
- Will I ever see my loved ones or friends who have died?

What God Wants Me to Know

1. No one can live forever on this earth. When Adam and Eve sinned, death and sickness entered the world. God told them that trials and suffering would also become part of life from then on.

2. People die in many ways, such as illnesses, accidents, and wars. People also die in natural disasters, such as tornados, earthquakes, fires and floods.

3. No one knows when or how they will die. God makes that decision.

4. Death is the separation of our spirit, or soul—who we are—from our body.

5. Our spirit goes to be where Jesus is, and our body is carefully buried in the ground in a cemetery.

6. We should not be afraid to die because God is with us. Jesus is with our spirits as they leave our bodies and go to live with Him.

7. When people we love die, we cry and grieve because we'll miss them very much. But Jesus assures us that we'll be together with our loved ones again in heaven.

8. The Bible says, "We will be with the Lord forever" (1 Thessalonians 4:17). These words comfort and encourage us when we are grieving.

Look at It This Way...

When Corrie ten Boom was a little girl growing up in Holland, she told her father she was afraid she would never be strong enough to die for Jesus Christ.

Her father said to her, "Tell me, when you take a train trip from Haarlem to Amsterdam, when do I give you money for the ticket? Three weeks before?"

She answered, "No, Daddy, you give me the money for the ticket just before we get on the train."

"That's right," her father replied, "and so it is with God's strength. Our wise Father in heaven knows when you are going to need things too...He will supply the strength you need—just in time."

Prayer

Dear God,

I know that You love me and have promised to be with me always. Help me to trust that You have a good plan for my life regardless of what happens to me and my family. I know that even when I die someday, I'll be with You forever. Amen.

Heaven

John 14:1-3

Do not let not your hearts be troubled. You believe in God; believe also in me. My Father's house has many rooms; if that were not so, would I have told you that I am going there to prepare a place for you? And if I go and prepare a place for you, I will come back and take you to be with me that you also may be where I am.

Revelation 21:1,27

Then I saw "a new heaven and a new earth," for the first heaven and the first earth had passed away, and there was no longer any sea...Nothing impure will ever enter [the new Jerusalem], nor will anyone who does what is shameful or deceitful, but only those whose names are written in the Lamb's book of life.

Heaven is where God lives in splendor and holiness. It is a real place, but it exists in a different kind of realm beyond the world and earth we live in. Heaven is where we go to live after we die if we have asked Jesus to forgive our sins and be our Savior. We will be completely happy there because we will be with Jesus forever.

What I Think

- Heaven seems like a fairy tale because it isn't part of this world.

- How can my body live in heaven?

- Will everyone go to heaven?

- Can I know for sure that I'll be with Jesus in heaven after I die?

What God Wants Me to Know

1. Heaven is a beautiful place God is preparing for people who love Him and try to obey Him. Everyone in heaven will worship God and serve Him in different ways.

2. Someday when you live in heaven, your body will be very different than it is now. It will be a special body, like Jesus's own body. It will be able to go through walls and move quickly from one place to another. You won't get tired or need to sleep.

3. There will be no sin, death, or tears in heaven. Nothing bad can happen there, and you will never do anything wrong. You will never get sick or hurt.

4. Some people don't love God, and they say mean and disrespectful things about Him. They will not live in heaven after they die.

5. This is how you can know for sure that someday you will live in heaven with Jesus—tell Him you know you are a sinner, ask Him to forgive your sins and be your Savior, thank Him

for dying on the cross for you, and tell Him you love Him and want to obey His rules in the Bible.

Look at It This Way...

One evening a mother read stories from a picture book about heaven to Anna, her eight-year-old daughter. That night Anna dreamed about heaven and about meeting Jesus. In the morning she told her mother, "I dreamed about meeting Jesus, and He is even more wonderful than the pictures!"

Prayer

Dear God,

Thank You for preparing a special place for me to live with You someday. I'm so glad that Jesus loves me and died on the cross for me. Please help me to love and obey You even when I don't want to. Amen.

Honesty

Proverbs 19:5
A false witness will not go unpunished, and whoever pours out lies will not go free.

Colossians 3:9-10
Do not lie to each other, since you have taken off your old self with its practices and have put on the new self, which is being renewed in knowledge in the image of its Creator.

1 John 1:8
If we claim to be without sin, we deceive ourselves and the truth is not in us.

Honesty is telling the truth even if we get embarrassed, rejected, made fun of...even if we get into trouble. If we tell a lie to hide our mistake or sin, we are usually afraid that someone will reject us. When we are not honest, we must accept the consequences of our actions.

What I Think

- When I disobey, I get scared and am tempted to lie about what I've done.

- Sometimes I really want to do something I'm not supposed to do, such as...

    spending time with a certain friend
    watching something on TV
    eating a certain food or snack
    taking something that belongs to someone else

What God Wants Me to Know

1. God cannot lie, and He doesn't want us to lie.

2. The devil is a liar and the father of lies (John 8:44).

3. The devil can speak to us in our minds/thoughts and lies to us. He wants us to sin and get into trouble.

4. Our own thoughts and desires can lead us to tell a lie.

5. Someone else may want you to tell a lie to cover up for them. Tell them no, and then talk to an adult whom you trust.

6. When we lie, others will not trust us. They won't know when we're telling the truth.

7. It is more important to tell the truth and go through the consequences, than to tell a lie.

8. When we choose to tell the truth, we are pleasing to God, and feel relieved and happy.

9. When we tell the truth, we can trust God to help us with whatever happens.

10. We must remember that God loves us and His way is the best.

Look at It This Way...

A teacher once told her students, "Today I'm giving you two tests—one in math and the other in honesty. I hope you will pass them both. If you must fail one, fail math. There are many good students who can't pass a test in math, but there are not many good people in the world who can't pass the test of honesty."

Prayer

Dear God,

When I'm tempted to tell a lie, please give me courage to tell the truth. I want to trust You to help me when I'm afraid of what will happen. Even more, help me to obey right away so I won't be tempted to lie to cover up my disobedience. Amen.

Prayer and Peace

Philippians 4:6-7

Do not be anxious about anything, but in every situation, by prayer and petition, with thanksgiving, present your requests to God. And the peace of God, which transcends all understanding, will guard your hearts and your minds in Christ Jesus.

Hebrews 4:16

Let us then approach God's throne of grace with confidence, so that we may receive mercy and find grace to help us in our time of need.

1 John 5:14-15

This is the confidence we have in approaching God: that if we ask anything according to his will, he hears us. And if we know that he hears us—whatever we ask—we know that we have what we asked of him.

Prayer is talking to God. It is taking time from the many things we could be doing to spend time with Him. Praying shows God that we love, trust, and need Him. Praying is a way to worship God because it shows Him that we believe He is important, wise, powerful, and good. When we pray, God can calm our thoughts and hearts and fill them with His peace.

What I Think

- How do I know that God hears my prayers?
- If I forget to pray, does God still love me?
- If God doesn't answer my prayers, does He still care about me?

What God Wants Me to Know

1. The Bible assures us that God hears and answers our prayers.

2. God has the power to do whatever He wants to when we pray and when we don't.

3. God wants us to talk to Him about what we need and want. When we don't pray, He still loves us, but we miss out on His help and blessing.

4. Our greatest need is to know God and to spend time with Him.

5. God allows us to experience various problems, sickness, and difficulties with other people so that we will talk to Him about them.

6. God doesn't want us to worry about all these things, but to pray about them.

7. God wants us to depend on Him for answers to our problems. He wants us to give our needs to Him and then be willing to accept whatever He gives us.

8. When God doesn't answer our prayers the way we want Him to, He still loves and cares about us. He knows everything, including what is best for us.

9. God changes our attitudes, wants, and desires when we pray. We learn to trust God no matter what happens or how He answers our prayers.

10. Praying and trusting God will bring His peace into our hearts and minds.

Look at It This Way...

When John F. Kennedy was president of the United States, his three-year-old son John often ran into his father's office without an appointment. In fact, pictures were taken of the little boy hiding beneath his father's desk in the Oval Office of the White House. Clearly, the president enjoyed having his son bounce into the room whenever he wanted.

God loves us just as a father loves his sons and daughters. He is delighted when we show up to tell Him about our needs and to ask for His help. When we pray we don't only ask God for things. We also learn to enjoy coming to Him, knowing that He looks forward to our visits more than we do.

Prayer

Dear God,

I'm so glad I can pray and talk to You just like this! Please help me to remember to pray and not to worry about anything. Even when I don't get what I want, I know You love me and care about me. You are a great God. Amen.

Accepting Ourselves

1 Samuel 16:7
The LORD does not look at the things people look at. People look at the outward appearance, but the LORD looks at the heart.

Psalm 139:13-14,16
You created my inmost being; you knit me together in my mother's womb. I praise you because I am fearfully and wonderfully made; your works are wonderful, I know that full well...Your eyes saw my unformed body; all the days ordained for me were written in your book before one of them came to be.

When we accept ourselves, we are content with the way we look and the abilities God has given us. We believe God created us the way we are and that it's all right to look different from someone else. When we accept ourselves, we can more easily accept others who don't look like us.

What I Think

- In my school, the cute and smart kids get more attention.
- No one seems to notice me.
- Some kids dress and act in bad ways to get attention.
- The television programs I watch all show funny, smart, and good-looking kids.

What God Wants Me to Know

1. Your value as a person comes from God, not from your looks, your skin color, or the country you were born in.
2. God gave you to your parents, and you look similar to them.
3. Before you were born, God planned and formed the body you now have.
4. You are special. No one in all the world looks exactly like you do.
5. You should not try to look like someone else.
6. God loves you just as He created you to be.
7. When you look in the mirror, you can thank God that He made you just the way you are.
8. The kind of character you have is more important than whether others think you are good looking.

Look at It This Way...

In his book *What Kids Need Most in a Dad*, Tim Hansel tells a story about a teenager who had a very obvious birthmark on much of his face. Despite this, he accepted himself just as he was, and as a result, he got along well with other students and was well liked. He had no self-consciousness about his appearance. Someone asked him how this could be.

He smiled and said, "When I was very young, my father

started telling me that the birth-mark was where an angel kissed me so my father could always find me easily in a crowd. My dad told me this so many times with so much love that as I grew up, I actually began to feel sorry for other kids who were not kissed by an angel like I was."*

Of course his dad knew that his son was not actually kissed by an angel, but this was the father's way of saying that despite his visible birthmark, he could accept it as a gift from his heavenly Father. He was just as loved and precious to God as the other children. Others might judge us by our appearance, but God looks in our hearts, and that is really what matters to Him.

Prayer

Dear God,

Sometimes I wish I looked different and could be as smart and popular as some of my friends. Please help me accept that I am the person You created me to be, and I don't need to try to be like someone else. Amen.

---

* Tim Hansel, *What Kids Need Most in a Dad* (Tarrytown, NY: Revell, 1989), p.75.

Getting Along with Others

Proverbs 15:1
A gentle answer turns away wrath, but a harsh word stirs up anger.

Romans 12:17-18
Do not repay anyone evil for evil. Be careful to do what is right in the eyes of everyone. If it is possible, as far as it depends on you, live at peace with everyone.

Ephesians 4:32
Be kind and compassionate to one another, forgiving each other, just as in Christ God forgave you.

1 John 4:11
Dear friends, since God so loved us, we also ought to love one another.

Getting along with others is not always easy, but it is one of the most important lessons we can learn. That is why God has given us many instructions about how to behave when others are difficult or they mistreat us. God wants us to live in peace and harmony. Jesus is our example, and He tells us how we can do it.

What I Think

- Does God know how hard it is for me to get along with my brother?

- I try to get along with my sister, but she is always picking on me.

- My parents blame me when things go wrong.

- I try to help my friends get along with each other.

What God Wants Me to Know

1. Getting along with others is hard work. We are all different from each other, and we are selfish. We want to be first, we want the best and the biggest for ourselves, and we don't like to share.

2. Sometimes we say mean things to others or about others in order to make ourselves feel or look better than them.

3. Jesus gave us a simple principle to follow called the Golden Rule: "So in everything, do to others what you would have them do to you" (Matthew 7:12). It trains us to control our actions, words, thoughts, and emotions.

4. We can get along with others by...

   > giving gentle answers, which turn away anger
   > refusing to argue
   > being patient and overlooking offenses
   > being kind and helpful
   > forgiving others just as God has forgiven us

refusing to be mean when others are mean to us
speaking with respect to everyone
living at peace with everyone
loving each other because God loves us

Look at It This Way...

In school Rachel tried to avoid a girl who teased her and told lies about her. Sometimes Rachel even had to run into the washroom to cry because she felt so angry and helpless when this girl was mean to her.

One day as Rachel was walking to school, she noticed that the girl who mistreated her accidently dropped her purse on the side-

walk but just kept on walking with her group of friends.

Rachel had to make a decision—should she leave the purse on the sidewalk? Rachel remembered that the Bible says we should be kind to our enemies, so she picked up the purse and carried it to school. Then she went to the girl's locker and said, "You dropped your purse this morning."

The girl didn't say anything. But from that time on she treated Rachel like one of her friends and never told lies about her again.

Prayer

Dear God,

It isn't easy for me to be kind, patient, and loving to people who are hard to get along with. I need Your help to treat others the way I want them to treat me. Help me to remember to do the right thing at the right time. Amen.

Jesus's Return

Acts 1:11
Men of Galilee...why do you stand here looking into the sky? This same Jesus, who has been taken from you into heaven, will come back in the same way you have seen him go into heaven.

1 Thessalonians 4:16
The Lord himself will come down from heaven, with a loud command, with the voice of the arch-angel and with the trumpet call of God, and the dead in Christ will rise first.

Revelation 1:7
Look, he is coming with the clouds...every eye will see him, even those who pierced Him.

Someday, Jesus will return to the earth, where He was born, lived, died, and rose again. No one knows when He will come back. Jesus told us that certain things will take place before He returns. Some of those things have happened, but some have not, so we don't know when He will return.

What I Think

- This is exciting!
- I love Jesus and want Him to come back soon.
- I wish everyone could go to heaven with Jesus.

What God Wants Me to Know

1. Jesus will return to earth two times. The first time is called the rapture. The second time is called the second coming.

2. When Jesus returns at the rapture...
   - Only God knows when this will happen.
   - It will be very exciting for those who know and love Him, and everyone will recognize Jesus!
   - Those believers who have died will be raised to life.
   - We will all have new bodies and go to live with Jesus.
   - People who don't love Jesus will be left on the earth.

3. When Jesus returns at the second coming...
   - The Bible tells us that Jesus will return seven years after the rapture.
   - There will be a great war on the earth between Jesus and His enemies, and Jesus will be the winner.
   - All of the injustices of the world will be made right as Jesus judges all the unbelievers.
   - He will rule as King on the earth.
   - All the children of the world and all the believers from the beginning of the world will live in heaven with Jesus forever.

Look at It This Way...

There was once an old farmer who had a very special pet dog. Whenever the farmer was working, the dog was right beside him and even helped him keep the other animals where they were supposed to be.

One day, the farmer died. He had left instructions for his family that he wanted to be buried near the place of his birth, which was a long way away. So his family carefully laid his body in a coffin and put it on a train.

The next day, the farmer's dog returned to the train station. In fact, the dog went to the train station every day, hoping that the train that took his master away would someday bring him back.

In the same way, the more we love Jesus, the more we will look forward to His return.

Prayer

Dear Jesus,

I hope You come back soon because I do love You. Help me to live in such a way that when You do come back, I will be ready. Also, help me to tell others about You so that they also will be ready when You return. Amen.

More Great Harvest House Books You Will Enjoy

Discover 4 Yourself®
Inductive Bible Studies for Kids
Kay Arthur and Janna Arndt

Bible study is serious fun! The studies in the *Discover 4 Yourself®* series help you find out for yourself what the Bible is all about—and give you exciting ways to do it! These hands-on books help teach you the basic skills of Bible study and prepare you for a lifetime of discovering God's Word.

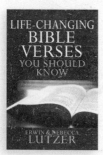

Just Mom and Me Having Tea
Mary J. Murray

Just Mom and Me Having Tea is a perfect venue for mothers and daughters to strengthen their special bond and grow in their Christian walk. Flexible lessons chock-full of creative ideas and activities cover topics important to girls ages six to nine.

Life-Changing Bible Verses You Should Know
Erwin and Rebecca Lutzer

Erwin Lutzer, senior pastor of The Moody Church, and his wife, Rebecca, encourage you to reap the blessings of memorizing Scripture in this gathering of relevant verses, 35 topics, insightful explanations, and engaging questions. This foundation of wisdom will inspire you to experience God's Word in powerful ways.